T0014392

RACCOONS
at Night

Kathleen A. Klatte

PowerKiDS
press.
New York

Published in 2021 by The Rosen Publishing Group, Inc.
29 East 21st Street, New York, NY 10010

First Edition

Portions of this work were originally authored by Doreen Gonzales and published as *Raccoons in the Dark*. All new material this edition authored by Kathleen A. Klatte.

Editor: Kathleen Klatte
Book Design: Michael Flynn

Photo Credits: Cover Eric Isselee/Shutterstock.com; (series background) MoreThanPicture/Shutterstock.com; p. 4 Will Rodrigues/Shutterstock.com; p. 5 Scenic Shutterbug/Shutterstock.com; pp. 7, 15 Landshark1/Shutterstock.com; p. 9 Farzad Darabi/Shutterstock.com; p. 10 Edwin Butter/Shutterstock.com; p. 11 James R Poston/Shutterstock.com; p. 12 Peter K. Ziminski/Shutterstock.com; p. 13 Gerald A. DeBoer/Shutterstock.com; p. 16 Anton Rogozin/Shutterstock.com; p. 17 Iza Korwel/Shutterstock.com; p. 19 Laurien Rose/Shutterstock.com; p. 21 Colin Woods/Shutterstock.com; p. 22 Sonsedska Yuliia/Shutterstock.com.

Library of Congress Cataloging-in-Publication Data

Names: Klatte, Kathleen A., author.
Title: Raccoons at night / Kathleen A. Klatte.
Description: New York : PowerKids Press, [2021] | Series: Up all night! nocturnal animals | Includes index.
Identifiers: LCCN 2019048843 | ISBN 9781725318779 (paperback) | ISBN 9781725318793 (library binding) | ISBN 9781725318786 (6 pack)
Subjects: LCSH: Raccoon–Juvenile literature. | Nocturnal animals–Juvenile literature.
Classification: LCC QL737.C26 K59 2021 | DDC 599.76/32–dc23
LC record available at https://lccn.loc.gov/2019048843

Some of the images in this book illustrate individuals who are models. The depictions do not imply actual situations or events.

Manufactured in the United States of America

CPSIA Compliance Information: Batch #CSPK20. For Further Information contact Rosen Publishing, New York, New York at 1-800-237-9932.

CONTENTS

CLEVER CRITTERS

Raccoons are clever and **adaptable** animals. Sometimes people get mad when raccoons are smart enough to get into their trash cans and coolers. Raccoons are nocturnal, which means they're active mainly at night. After the sun goes down, they come out of their dens to find food.

THIS TRASH CAN WAS PROBABLY COVERED, BUT HUNGRY RACCOONS WILL STOP AT NOTHING TO FIND THEIR DINNER.

WHILE YOU'RE SLEEPING

There's a very common belief that raccoons out in daylight must be sick. You should never approach any wild animal, but a raccoon that looks and acts healthy is most likely just **foraging** for food.

The North American raccoon is a furry **mammal** that may live in a range from northern Canada down to South America. They often live in wooded areas near water. Many raccoons make their dens in hollow logs, rocks, and the old **burrows** of other animals. Some raccoons live under decks or in **abandoned** buildings. Raccoons may even make their homes in people's houses.

MASKS AND MARKINGS

Raccoons are about the size of small dogs. They can weigh about 22 pounds (10 kg) or more and measure 30 to 36 inches (76.2 to 91.4 cm) long. Raccoons have gray or brown fur. They have long, bushy tails with several dark rings. These colors and markings help hide raccoons when they're out at night.

Raccoons have small ears that stand up on their heads. These mammals also have wide faces with pointed noses. Raccoons are known for the bands of dark fur around their eyes. These dark stripes are often called masks. Raccoons can recognize one another by their masks.

RACCOONS ARE VERY CLEVER AT OPENING DOORS AND GETTING INTO SMALL PLACES. THEY CAN MAKE AN AWFUL MESS IF THEY GET INSIDE YOUR HOME.

HELPFUL HANDS

A raccoon's natural **habitat** is woodland. They have long claws on each of their paws that help them climb. Raccoons are good climbers and can even move down trees headfirst.

Raccoons have handlike front paws that are very **sensitive**. They use these paws to hold and feel things. Raccoons can tell if something is good to eat by feeling it. Their paws help them hunt in the dark. Raccoons also use them to move objects around. They can open doors and take the lids off trash cans. Their sensitive paws and clever brains allow them to cause a great deal of trouble!

RACCOONS' FRONT PAWS ARE VERY SIMILAR TO HUMAN HANDS. THEY OFTEN LEAVE WHAT LOOK LIKE DIRTY, CHILD-SIZE HANDPRINTS ON THINGS THEY'VE TRIED TO OPEN.

9

EVERYTHING'S ON THE MENU

Raccoons will eat just about anything. They're often called **carnivores** but are actually **omnivores**. These masked mammals like eating crabs, bird eggs, frogs, fish, mice, corn, fruit, nuts, seeds, and grasshoppers.

Raccoons are good at finding food in the dark. They can see well in darkness because their eyes take in lots of light. Raccoons also use their excellent hearing and sense of smell to find food at night. Many raccoons can even smell nuts or mice that are under the ground! Raccoons use touch to find food in the dark, too. They will use their front paws to reach for fish or other small water animals.

11

MIDNIGHT SNACKING

Raccoons tend to be most active after dark. They generally walk toward the nearest lake or stream, stopping along the way to look for food. If they don't find enough food before they get to the water, raccoons begin fishing there.

WHILE YOU'RE SLEEPING

Raccoons don't really wash their food before eating it. They just tend to hunt around water and eat things that they catch there.

ALTHOUGH PEOPLE IN CITY AREAS ARE MOST FAMILIAR WITH RACCOONS EATING TRASH OR STEALING PET FOOD, RACCOONS IN THE WILD WILL EAT WHATEVER THEY CAN FIND OR CATCH.

Although raccoons prefer nighttime, there are reasons they'll come out during the day. A nursing mother who's very hungry might come out in search of more food. Raccoons who learn of a food source, such as cafeteria trash being put out at a certain time, will also take advantage of the chance for a meal.

FAMILY LIFE

Raccoons in the wild often make dens in hollow trees or logs. Raccoons that live in cities will den in places such as in sheds, under decks, or even in attics if they can find a way inside. Male raccoons tend to live alone for most of the year, while females live with their young.

Raccoons that live in places where the weather gets cold sometimes share a den with other raccoons during the winter. This helps them keep warm. In the winter, raccoons spend much of their time sleeping. To prepare for winter, raccoons will eat plenty of food and increase their body fat.

WHILE YOU'RE SLEEPING

Raccoons can communicate with each other through a wide variety of calls and sounds. They can chitter, purr, or whimper. They might growl or snarl to warn another animal away.

A HOLLOW TREE OR ABANDONED BEAVER LODGE MAKES A GOOD HOME FOR RACCOONS. THEY CAN CAUSE A GREAT DEAL OF TROUBLE TRYING TO FIND A WAY INSIDE A BUILDING.

A NURSERY OF RACCOONS

Did you know that a group of raccoons is sometimes called a nursery? Female raccoons generally give birth to three or four babies in spring, after being pregnant for about two months. Newborn raccoons, or kits, weigh 3 to 5 ounces (85 to 141.7 g). They don't open their eyes until they're 20 days old. Kits drink their mother's milk for about two months.

RACCOONS IN **CAPTIVITY** CAN LIVE UP TO 20 YEARS, BUT RACCOONS IN THE WILD SELDOM LIVE FIVE YEARS. SOME BABIES DON'T BUILD UP ENOUGH BODY FAT TO SURVIVE THEIR FIRST WINTER.

At five months of age, young raccoons begin going out with their mothers at night. Mother raccoons teach their young how to find food and stay safe. Young raccoons stay with their mothers for about a year. Mother raccoons are very protective of their babies, even after they start to forage for themselves.

DANGER IN THE NIGHT

One of the ways that raccoons keep safe is by sleeping in their den during the day. However, a few nocturnal hunters, such as coyotes, wolves, and owls, do hunt raccoons. Raccoons know this, so they stay watchful when they're out at night. They listen carefully for animals that might try to catch them.

When predators come too close, raccoons often try to scare them away. The raccoons hiss, growl, and show their teeth. If they need to, raccoons will even fight predators with their claws and teeth. Raccoons can also escape by swimming or climbing away.

WHILE YOU'RE SLEEPING

Humans are responsible for the deaths of many raccoons. In some places, raccoons are hunted for their fur or meat. It's also common to see a raccoon that's been hit by a car.

IN THE PAST, RACCOON-FUR COATS WERE SO VALUABLE THAT RACCOONS WERE TAKEN TO PLACES IN EUROPE. THERE, THEY'VE CAUSED PROBLEMS FOR PEOPLE AND NATIVE ANIMAL SPECIES.

MAKING THEMSELVES AT HOME

Raccoons are very quick to adapt to changes in their habitat. If the woods they live in are cut down, raccoons find new places to live. When raccoons can't find the kinds of food they're used to, they try new foods. In fact, raccoons will eat just about anything. For these reasons, raccoons are happy living in many different places.

These smart mammals often live in towns and cities, near people. People who have raccoons living around them need to be careful, though. Raccoons can have **parasites** such as fleas and ticks. They also carry serious diseases that people and pets might catch.

A WILDLIFE SPECIALIST CAUGHT THIS RACCOON IN A TRAP. THE TRAP WON'T HURT IT, AND THE SPECIALIST CAN SAFELY TAKE THE RACCOON OUT TO THE WOODS TO BE RELEASED.

PEOPLE AND RACCOONS

Even though they sometimes live very close to people, it's important to remember that raccoons are wild animals. Some raccoons eat crops, such as corn, that are growing on farms. Raccoons have also been known to get into gardens and eat fish from backyard ponds. At times, raccoons even get into houses and make a mess.

There are companies that work to remove raccoons from places where they don't belong. Even so, the number of raccoons is growing in many areas. As Earth's climate continues to change, and people keep clearing woodlands, raccoons will find new places to live.

GLOSSARY

abandoned: Left to fall into a state of disuse.

adaptable: Able to change in order to live better in certain environments.

burrow: A hole an animal digs in the ground for shelter.

captivity: For an animal, the state of living somewhere controlled by humans—such as in a zoo or an aquarium—instead of in the wild.

carnivore: An animal that eats only meat.

forage: To search for something (such as food or supplies).

habitat: The natural home for plants, animals, and other living things.

mammal: A warm-blooded animal that has a backbone and hair, breathes air, and feeds milk to its young.

omnivore: An animal that eats both plants and other animals.

parasite: A living thing that lives in, on, or with another living thing and often harms it.

sensitive: Able to sense very small changes in something.

INDEX

WEBSITES

Due to the changing nature of Internet links, PowerKids Press has developed an online list
of websites related to the subject of this book. This site is updated regularly. Please use this
link to access the list: www.powerkidslinks.com/uan/raccoons